Haiku for a Season ❋ Haiku per una stagione

haiku

for a season | per una stagione

Andrea Zanzotto

Edited by Anna Secco and Patrick Barron

THE UNIVERSITY OF CHICAGO PRESS   CHICAGO AND LONDON

The University of Chicago Press, Chicago 60637
The University of Chicago Press, Ltd., London
English texts and compilation © 2012 by
The University of Chicago
All rights reserved. Published 2012.
Printed in the United States of America

21 20 19 18 17 16 15 14 13 12   1 2 3 4 5

ANDREA ZANZOTTO
(1921–2011) was the
author of more than
twenty books of
poems and collections
of prose, including
*The Selected Poetry and
Prose of Andrea Zan-
zotto*, also published
by the University of
Chicago Press.

PATRICK BARRON
is associate professor
of English at the
University of Massa-
chusetts Boston.

ANNA SECCO
is an independent
scholar and translator
of numerous articles,
essays, and short
works from English
into Italian.

This paper meets
the requirements of
ANSI/NISO Z39.48-
1992 (Permanence
of Paper).

ISBN-13: 978-0-226-92221-8 (paper)
ISBN-13: 978-0-226-92222-5 (e-book)
ISBN-10: 0-226-92221-9 (paper)
ISBN-10: 0-226-92222-7 (e-book)

*The University of Chicago Press gratefully acknowledges the
generous financial support of the Italian Ministry of Foreign
Affairs, through the Italian Cultural Institute of Chicago,
toward the publication of this book.*

*La University of Chicago Press ringrazia il Ministero degli
Affari Esteri italiano per il generoso sostegno finanziario
fornito, tramite l'Istituto Italiano di Cultura di Chicago, alla
pubblicazione di questo libro.*

Autograph on p. iv: Courtesy of Andrea Zanzotto.

Library of Congress Cataloging-in-Publication Data
Zanzotto, Andrea, 1921–2011
Haiku for a season = Haiku per una stagione / Andrea
Zanzotto ; edited by Anna Secco and Patrick Barron.
pages ; cm.
English and Italian.
Includes bibliographical references and index.
ISBN 978-0-226-92221-8 (paperback : alkaline paper) —
ISBN 0-226-92221-9 (paperback : alkaline paper) —
ISBN 978-0-226-92222-5 (e-book) — ISBN 0-226-92222-7
(e-book)
I. Title. II. Title: Haiku per una stagione.
PQ4851.A74H35   2012
851'.914—dc23   2012003675

Contents

Parallel worlds, roots
of vitreous deep languages –
bubbles weep in throats

Editors' Note

The short lyrics collected in *Haiku for a Season*, composed
in English during the spring and summer of 1984 and pub-
lished here for the first time, are concentrated musings on
humble, oftentimes ephemeral aspects of the landscape,
from subtle shifts in capricious spring weather to the antics
of vivid wild plants. They are windows into varyingly playful,
restless, and meditative emotive states, as well as linguistic
experiments that mark a shift in Zanzotto's work toward the
fragmentary and condensed, evident in all three of his most
recent volumes, *Meteo* (Weather report, 1996), *Sovrimpressioni*
(Suprimpressions, 2001), and *Conglomerati* (Conglomerates,
2009). The collection is a rather unusual addition to Zanzot-
to's opus in that while he has often made use of other lan-
guages, never has he done so to the extent presented here in
a systematic experiment with bilingual poetry. The poems—
or "pseudo-haiku" as Zanzotto refers to them—do not fol-
low the traditional form of seventeen syllables divided into
three lines of five–seven–five, and as such, loosely resemble
haiku instead of adhere to any formal structure. They seem
rather "uncertain fragments," as Zanzotto calls the closely
related poems in *Meteo*, that like the soft filaments of float-
ing seeds, register "faint laments faraway / vibratile traps

capturing the falling light."[1] These "downy incertitudes" and "mystic mini-anemometers" scattered throughout the collection, beseech as much as they proffer, whisper as well as sing.[2]

Zanzotto's minimalist, experimental English holds many unexpected twists in syntax and condensations of image and action. Long interested in the origins and transformations of language, Zanzotto has throughout his career sought out linguistic nexuses where language comes into its own, taking originary, shifting form from the force of primal utterance in one instance, just as moments later it threatens to metamorphose into some new idiom under the pressure of hyper-sophistication. The haphazard, inventive babbling of young children, glosses from the work of venerated or unknown poets, scientific jargon, dialectal expressions, invented words, jingles from commercials, and common speech appear throughout his work, which has evolved through a series of periods of experimentation—from early hermetic- and symbolist-influenced verse that celebrates and seeks relief in natural beauty, to later increasingly decentered work that laments the landscape's despoilment as it evinces suspicion over the authenticity and reliability of language, to more recent poetry that confronts lasting degradations in both the external world and the very concept of nature. *Haiku for a Season* fits well within this trajectory, offering further iterations, tinkerings with possible new dialects, ever more "breaths of shadow," "minitalks," and "sh-shining tics."[3]

1. Andrea Zanzotto, *The Selected Poetry and Prose of Andrea Zanzotto* (Chicago: University of Chicago Press, 2007), 285; translated from *Meteo* (Rome: Donzelli, 1996), 15.
2. See pages 30 and 72.   3. See pages 2, 20, and 6.

Our edits to the texts, done in close collaboration with Zanzotto over a number of years before his death in October 2011, are limited to occasional minor adjustments to word choice or syntax, allowing for playful, minor violations of grammar and usage to stand as integral to the poems' idiosyncratic, nonnative vitality. The Italian versions were composed by Zanzotto at intervals many years after the English texts, and should be considered as roughly parallel, yet not always precise, renditions of the English originals. At times they function as semiautonomous texts, clearly invoking the originals, yet also indicating new directions and meanings. The reversals of expected process in the bilingual composition of *Haiku for a Season* at once complicate the unfolding of meaning in the English and Italian versions, yet also underscore the texts' interdependence.

The collection ends with an essay on the haiku form that Zanzotto wrote as an introduction for a 1982 Italian collection of haiku in translation, *Cento haiku* (One hundred haiku). The essay celebrates the beauty and mystery of the haiku, eloquently arguing for its universality while also warning of the difficulty of co-opting it, even when careful homage is paid to its origins. And yet it seems to us that in *Haiku for a Season* he succeeds in embracing the form's "nearly precultural physicality" and "primordial biorhythms" by the seemingly paradoxical use of a language not his own.[4] Attempting to touch the archaic processes of the psyche that unite language to nature, Zanzotto generously, if minimally, offers us compelling glimpses of "a vague lack, a sweetly ritualized throbbing, the nonsound of the sense that opens into and embraces the nonsense of nature," one step, verse, and season at a time.[5]

4. See page 98.   5. See page 99.

Haiku for a Season ❀ Haiku per una stagione

I grew in a thousand
breaths of shadow
but I didn't forget

❊

In April-pink
I arise when
in sunset it sinks

Sono cresciuto tra mille
soffi di ombre
ma non lo posso dimenticare

＊

Nel rosa-aprile
mi risveglio quando
nel tramonto affonda

Borderline of street-lamps
with a touching awareness
sparing a moon-flash

❖

Please: this pink iris
Please: these hot drops
"Please," that harmonizes all

4

Profilo di lampioni
con una toccante consapevolezza
che salva un flash di luna

❖

Per favore: questo iris rosa
Per favore: queste gocce calde
"Per favore," che tutto armonizza

The bough caresses
or whips aprilities:
the withdrawal of nothing
made sh-shining tics

*

In reticent spring skies
autumnal leaves, fragments
of far future events

Il ramo accarezza
o stimola aprilità:
il ritirarsi di niente
reso balbettìi lucenti

*

Nei reticenti cieli di primavera
foglie autunnali, frammenti
di remoti futuri eventi

An interior world-fog generates
frogs and rotten foods
swift fires of eyes burn it all

❊

Beyond violet and pink gates:
all eternal exhalation—
Pull them push them

Una nebbia dentro al mondo ranocchi
genera, e cibo marcio
poi fuochi di occhi pungenti bruciano tutto

    *

Tutto si vide attraverso cancelli
violetti e rosa, eterna esalazione—
tirali spingili

Seeking a way out
through some tricky ants
which cram a mindful sunshine

❁

A man said "Don't weave mist"—
this weaving—yet his filaments
everywhere vanishing—
in dazzling memories turn, twist

Cercando una via d'uscita
fra formiche truffaldine
che ammucchiano una densa solarità

*

Qualcuno disse "No filar caivo"—
questo tessere—pur i suoi filamenti
evanescenti ovunque—
mutano, girano in memorie splendenti

Thin start of the valley
beyond breathing peach-trees
"discovers" thin honey

❧

Gray wind, dust
still flowering
in absent-minded clouds

Stretto inizio della vallata
dietro peschi respiranti
"scopre" un miele sottile

*

Grigio vento, polvere
ancora fiorente
in nuvole distratte

Rocky blue in the north
and astonishing ice-dreams
tail of worried winter

❄

Tricky snow in May
pricking skins hairs roses
and frozen noses

Roccioso blu a nord
e stupefacenti sogni di ghiaccio
coda di un inverno pauroso

*

Neve truffaldina di maggio
punge pelli capelli rose
e nasi congelati

Yellow joy,
blackbird pecking in the meadow
grains of dawn

❖

Petals pappi cotton-filaments
noses in sneezes awakening
all is allergy

Gialla gioia,
il merlo becchetta nel prato
grani d'alba

＊

Petali soffioni filamenti
nasi si svegliano in sternuti
tutto è allergia

"No more May" they say
in blue and gray
secret insects secret hails

*

Powder of lost battles
between blue and green
when skylines weigh on grass

In blu e in grigio
"niente più maggio" dicono
segreti insetti grandini segrete[1]

✣

Polvere di passate perdute battaglie
tra blu e verde
quando gli orizzonti pesano sull'erba

1. For variants of this and a number of other poems in
this collection, see "Leggende," in *Meteo*, 23–24.

Lost-shy petals on panes,
clipped minitalks, past thoughts—
little bitter teeth biting

*

Parallel worlds, roots
of vitreous deep languages—
bubbles weep in throats

Timidi-perduti petali sui vetri
mini-discorsi spezzettati, pensieri passati—
mordenti asprigni dentini

❋

Mondi paralleli, radici
di vitrei profondi linguaggi—
bolle piangono in gole

Never-lacking snow of half-May
whom do you wish to save
whom do you insist on saving?

❖

In misty afternoon depths
"nevertheless, nevertheless"
trembling needles

Mai mancante neve di metà maggio
chi vuoi salvare
chi insisti nel salvare?

✽

Nella profondità nebbiosa del pomeriggio
"però, però"
tremanti aghi

Waves of mist and certitude
in a remote silver paddle:
nearing, nearing memory

      *

Fruits or flowers of light
on the dirty crazy stem
of the derrick in the night—
disloyalty to fireflies

Onde di nebbia e certezza
in una remota pagaia d'argento:
arriva, arriva la memoria

✽

Frutti o fiori di luce
sullo stelo sudicio e pazzo
della gru nella notte—
slealtà verso le lucciole

What, why the dirtiest May
of the century—a hundred
years of darkness in a month?

✻

Thin voices, bewildered bees and hopes—
everything dreams of other journeys
everything returns in little thick cuts

Come, perché il maggio più cupo
del secolo—cent'anni
di oscurità in un mese?

✻

Voci sottili, sconcertate api e speranze—
tutto sogna di altri viaggi
tutto ritorna in piccoli fitti tagli

Grass, larks and weak sun—
who sighs and sneezes?
So much soot in throats?

✣

Thunder like knots and knuckles
when pink roots from the skies
give us cracked walnuts

Erba, allodole e un sole debole—
chi sospira e sternuta?
Come mai tanta fuliggine nelle gole?

     *

Tuoni come nodi e nocche
quando radici rosa dai cieli
ci donano noci schiacciate

Downy incertitudes, gray
on gray, but crickets
multiply reflections in the display

❊

Delicate makeup of silk
in reflections of far distances—
all simple thought is near

Lanuginose incertezze, grigie
e grigie, ma i grilli
moltiplicano riflessi nel display

✻

Delicato belletto di seta
nel riflesso di grandi distanze—
ogni pensiero semplice è vicino

"I find I find oh I find"—
 silky yes of rain still beloved
 still self-replaying yes

     ✹

On the birthday of May
"Thou art not omnipotent"
 the pale girl-child says

"Trovo trovo oh io trovo"—
serico sì di pioggia ancora tanto amata
un sì che si ripete ancora

*

Nel compleanno del maggio
"Tu non sei onnipotente"
dice la pallida fanciulla

No madness but sweetness in a distance
measured by a door ajar—
meadows treasure up a thousand freedoms

❊

Challenge of the firefly
nevermore dead—forever
forgotten smile of Pasolini[2]

2. See Pier Paolo Pasolini, "'Il Vuoto del potere' ovvero
'L'Articolo delle lucciole,'" in *Scritti Corsari* (Milan:
Garzanti, 1975), 160–68.

Non follia ma dolcezza in lontananza
misurata da una porta socchiusa—
i prati tesorizzano mille libertà

❋

Sfida della lucciola
giammai morta—per sempre
obliato sorriso di Pasolini

It is fine to accept all challenges
of evanescent colors, seeing
behind, issuing all challenges

*

Aims and wishes faintly felt
violet of pansies
under eyes and eyes
dazzled eyes, when May denies

Va bene accettare tutte le sfide
di colori evanescenti, vedere
dietro, provocare tutte le sfide

*

Mete e desideri appena sentiti,
violetto di pansé
dietro sguardi e sguardi
sconcertati sguardi, quando maggio si nega

Maybe bees of ice in subtle
inaudible swarms behind the clouds—
not persuaded, a thin bough nods

*

Hail, hailstones like cruel snow—
an estranged promise spreads,
on wounded leaves, on closed paths

Forse api di ghiaccio in sottili
sciami impercettibili dietro le nuvole—
non convinto un gracile ramo annuisce

❁

Grandine, chicchi come neve crudele—
una promessa aliena si sparge,
su foglie ferite, su chiusi sentieri

The hail-kid, frozen but
rising May: "I am not
omnipotent," on the roofs he raps

❂

Vain threat of nervous rain—
a spider weaves far greater
examples of courage

Il ragazzo grandine, congelato ma
risorgente maggio: "Non sono
onnipotente," sui tetti batte

❋

Vana minaccia di pioggia nervosa—
un ragno tesse ben altri
esempi di coraggio

Snow-hail sooty skies mixes—
but the rare and radiant maid says:[3]
"never as now have blossomings been seen
destined for different times"

❋

At long last vanishes
the fiercest May of the millennium—
its misshapen sun
suffers the knife-eclipse too

3. For this and other references to the "rare and radi-
ant maiden," see Edgar Allan Poe's "The Raven."

Neve-grandine cieli scuri rimescola—
ma la rara e raggiante fanciulla dice:
"mai come ora si son viste fioriture
destinate a tempi diversi"

❊

Finalmente svanisce
il maggio più feroce del millennio—
il suo sole deforme
sopporta anche l'accoltellante eclisse

Black-electric cloud-blanket:
no eye can espy the crimes
of eclipse against the sun

＊

Acid spray of sunset
acid roots on the horizon
acid: suddenly invented speeches

Cupo elettrico manto di nubi:
nessun occhio può spiare i crimini
dell'eclisse contro il sole

❋

Acida spruzzata del tramonto
acide radici all'orizzonte
acido: improvvisamente inventati linguaggi

The bad prophet with umbrella
goes away away shaking—
in a fairy-blue corner—
the gentle eclipse gently knifes the sun

*

Less and less do little hopes burn
more and more doubtful minutes
nobody here will know the event

Il cattivo profeta con l'ombrello
se ne va lungi lungi scuotendolo—
in un angolo blu fatato—
la gentile eclisse gentilmente accoltella il sole

*

Sempre meno le piccole speranze bruciano
sempre più dubbiosi si fanno i minuti
nessuno qui conoscerà il vero

Insight, if possible, into landscape
which has not yet quiet faiths—
insight, sigh now, tomorrow blue lack

*

Acid-funny storm of petals
freedom which opens
qualities of spaces—
nothing collides with anybody

Acuto sguardo, se possibile, entro il paesaggio
che non ha ancora fedi tranquille—
acuto sguardo, ora sospiro, domani vuoto blu

❋

Acida scherzosa tempesta di petali
libertà che apre
qualità di spazi—
niente collide con nessuno

Blessed instants, daisies
blessed poppy—self-assured—when
uncertain drops combing pass

＊

The meek-eyed, the path without
anxiety invites, persuades
you will be still and still and still

Beati istanti, margherite
beato papavero—certo di sé—quando
gocce incerte pettinando passano

❋

L'occhiata mansueta, il sentiero senza
ansietà invita, persuade
in silenzio, in silenzio starai

Tiredness of the bleeding
uninhabitable spring—
a stray dog scents the only passage

*

Within stars and trips
within gems and tears
an "I" remakes as a movie its "I"

Stanchezza della sanguinante
inabitabile primavera—
un cane vagabondo annusa l'unico passaggio

     *

Tra stelle e viaggi
tra gemme e lacrime
un "Io" rifà come film il suo "Io"

Furious smoky green of June
betrayal of the possible—
faithfulness and gift of all the impossible

     ✻

"Nevermore can we disappear"
the maid whom we guard
already hints:
that's talk of buried hills

Furioso fumoso verde di giugno
tradimento del possibile—
fedeltà e dono di tutto l'impossibile

❊

"Giammai possiamo scomparire"
la fanciulla che proteggiamo
ormai suggerisce:
questo è il linguaggio delle sepolte colline

Haiku of an unforeseen daybreak
maybe mine—maybe drawls
or mini-noises of other universes

*

Careless mini-dreamings blossom
or awakenings blossom
haiku at daybreak, pappi vainly pursued

Haiku di un'alba inattesa
forse mia—forse cenni
o sussurri di altri universi

*

Svagati sognolii sbocciano
o risvegli sbocciano
haiku all'alba, pappi invano inseguiti

Like glass sucked by its glamour,
glass frightening the rare maid
photophobias of nothing in nothing

❋

Hippy crowd against the rain,
poppy revolution—
where I was solitary-red
a red billion bangs

Come cristalli risucchiati dal loro fascino,
cristalli che turbano la rara fanciulla
fotofobie di nulla nel nulla

*

Folla hippy contro la pioggia,
rivoluzione di papaveri—
dove io ero solitario-rosso
un rosso miliardo esplode

Alone the poppy
that has lost my friends
his friends and me, poppies

     ✢

Oblivious red forgotten—
a poppy behind the eyes—
reading the green
by a thousand laugh-red rays

Un papavero solitario
che ha perduto i miei amici
i suoi amici e me, papaveri

*

Oblioso rosso dimenticato—
un papavero che legge il verde—
da dietro gli occhi
da un migliaio di raggi rosso ridenti

Poppies, no drops of innocent blood
no funny flashes of wheat:
wildly sweet the world kisses me

      *

Where, small weak troops,
and why and when? I seek vainly
you seek vainly the sites
of your shy brittle battle

Papaveri, non gocce di sangue innocente
nessun guizzo scherzoso nel tappeto di grano:
selvaggio e dolce mi bacia il mondo

*

Dove, piccole deboli truppe,
e perché e quando? Io cerco invano
voi cercate invano i luoghi
della vostra timida tenera battaglia

Poppy, absent smell, mental smell?
Why do you open wide your eye?
Why so alive, so only-alive?

❋

A kind of azure as in a nightmare
in the distance—where I sank—
poppies near me gently clap

Papavero, profumo assente, profumo mentale?
Perché spalanchi l'occhio?
Perché così vivo, unicamente vivo?

*

Un modo di azzurro come di un incubo
in lontananza—dove sprofondai—
papaveri vicino a me gentili applaudono

After the storm the wheat keeled over
the cherry-tree ruffled and robbed
only the poppy wins
and wins in the wind

❋

Who so slowly rides the radiant bike[4]
in far-wide meadows, on the boundaries?
Maybe he collected nuggets, maybe he knew

4. See "Squadrare il foglio / Squaring the Sheet," *The Selected Poetry and Prose of Andrea Zanzotto*, 222–25.

Dopo la tempesta il frumento inginocchiato
il ciliegio arruffato e derubato
solo il papavero vince
e vince nel vento

❊

Chi pedala così lentamente la bici raggiante
nei vasti prati lontani, là sui confini?
Forse cercava pepite, forse sapeva

Replaying the words of June
as if they were my own words
as if they were words of another June

     ❖

Drawing a poppy pulled up
in a firing-area too much alive to bear
drawings, shadows of itself

Risentendo le parole di giugno
come se fossero le mie stesse parole
come se fossero le parole di un altro giugno

❊

Dipingendo un papavero raccolto
in un campo di battaglia, troppo vivo per sopportare
disegni, ombre di se stesso

Mini-volcanoes, poppies down here up there,
gifts for worried oblivious hills—
for our oblivion, sweetest gifts

*

Merry topsails of wrecked
vessels in the wheat sea?
Poppies: rescues everywhere begin

Vulcanelli, papaveri qua e là,
doni per devastate dimenticate colline—
per la nostra dimenticanza, i doni più dolci

     ✻

Vele augurali di navi
naufragate nel mare di frumento?
Papaveri: salvataggi cominciano ovunque

Poppies, good fellows,
suddenly in clumps come out
to confirm the paths, to confirm
the tired rivulets in the hills

❄

A subtlest breeze the poppies reveal,
mystic mini-anemometers
my eventual self reveal

Papaveri, buoni compagni,
sbocciati improvvisi a gruppi
per confermare i sentieri, per confermare
gli stanchi piccoli rivi nelle colline

    ✻

Una sottilissima brezza rivelano i papaveri,
mistici mini-anemometri
il mio fragile io rivelano

The secret sister—maybe—of the maid
whom we quivering recognize
by her quivering—
from the poppies takes her eyes

          ✹

What a brightening open-handedness
what an impossibility
of failure—you poppies—all other kinds
of generosity, misborn, sick

La sorella segreta—forse—della fanciulla
che tremanti noi riconosciamo
dal suo tremore—
fuori dai papaveri lancia i suoi sguardi

    *

Che brillante apertura di mani
che impossibilità
di fallire—voi papaveri—ogni altra specie
di generosità nata male, malata

You, wind, trustful in ears
brother of skies—being a party
to all composition no decomposition

     ❧

Last poppies, thinly hemorrhagic
following other thoughts, distresses—
rich in virtues, humblenesses

Tu, vento, confidente dell'orecchio
fratello dei cieli—partecipe
di ogni composizione non scomposizione

    *

Ultimi papaveri, soavemente emorragici
seguaci di altri pensieri, tensioni—
ricchi di virtù ed umiltà

Still here? Even in the ravine, in the fault?
Even under the beak of cheerful hens?
Poppies, resurrections that naivety invents

※

A scuffle of poppies which together ran
towards the nearest sky in the grass—
each with its own target

Ancora qui? Anche nelle faglie, nella forra?
Anche sotto il becco di spettegolanti galline?
Papaveri, resurrezioni che l'innocenza inventa

※

Scalpiccìo di papaveri che corsero insieme
verso il cielo vicino che digrada nell'erba—
ognuno proteso verso la propria meta

Ripeness of winds which
spread everywhere thousands
and thousands of seeds of fantasy
red knowledge

❃

All is ripeness and more—
waters lights skies flowers bees—
the simple "I" wishes
to get into this star system

Maturità dei venti che
spargono ovunque mille
e mille semi di fantasia
sanguinea conoscenza

❋

Tutto è maturità e più—
acque luci cieli fiori api—
il semplice "io" anela
a far parte di questo "star system"

Gray-blue, lake, an appeasement in
the green, forest—disposed as addenda
of a sum that never ceases to avoid, to astound

❊

The lake is, at long last, only the lake
the nymphéas only nymphéas
no more signs there, no frightening pleonasms

Lago, grigio-blu, una pienezza nel
verde, foresta—disposta come addendi
di una somma che non cessa mai di evitare di stupire

❊

Il lago è, alla fine, solo il lago
le ninfee solo ninfee
non più segni là, nessun terrificante pleonasmo

Where is the power of the naughty girl?
I neither wish nor hope she may lightly play
she is only a flower in a bush—unknown—
a thorny but necessary eventuality

❀

No being of glory, sister of darkness
No being of any darkness anywhere—
summer-highness no more than

a virtue, a caress

Dov'è il potere della fanciulla streghina?
Non desidero ne spero che possa giocare leggera
è solo un fiore nella boscaglia—sconosciuto
una spinosa ma necessaria realtà

    ✻

Non essere della gloria, sorella della cupezza
Non essere di ogni cupezza in nessun luogo—
la pienezza dell'estate non più di
                una virtù, di una carezza

Joy of July, source of all joys
in the shape of haiku or, maybe, other poems—
sweetly, palely in nature
                    sleeps the writing

        ❋

The little volcano named July
lets flow a tender lava for everything—
let life be something
                    more than a dream

Gioia del luglio, fonte di ogni gioia
in forma di haiku o, forse, poemi—
dolcemente, pallidamente nella natura
                              dorme la scrittura

                    ❉

Il vulcanello di nome luglio
fa fluire una tenera lava verso ogni cosa—
che la vita sia qualcosa
                    di più di un sogno

Benefits of sleep—unthinkable—
sleep thick as the colors of the grass—
everything will gain immense wealth

❊

To be and not to be
dazzling eyes
in a claiming face
lips of a mouth crying "to be"

Vantaggi del sonno—inimmaginabili—
sonno denso come i colori dell'erba—
tutto guadagnerà immensa ricchezza

      *

Essere e non essere
occhi abbaglianti
in un viso che attira
labbra di una bocca che grida "essere"

Pen and ink insist across and beyond
shapes and frames of a brightening day
sweetly trying to feed on them
sweetly making plans

❀

Where poppies played
the sickle passed a hundred years ago—
now shy smell of grass remains:
oblivion, yet living oblivion

Penna e inchiostro insistono entro
forme e limiti di una brillante giornata
che tenta gentilmente di nutrirsi
gentilmente progettando

＊

Dove giocavano i papaveri
la falce passò un centinaio di anni fa—
ora timido resta l'odore dell'erba:
oblio, ma oblio vivente

Other meadows, wishes, feeling
in new star systems—the man
who avoided who threaded
comes riding his untiring bike

Altri prati, desideri, emozioni
in nuovi "star systems"—l'uomo
che sostò che intessé
avanza cavalcando la sua instancabile bici

Foreword to Cento haiku*

That the haiku seems to hold such great appeal outside of
the Japanese cultural matrix is a reminder of the need to
persistently return to its origins if we hope to understand
the form, however approximately. The erasure of ideograms
and their flowerings, a casualty of translation, evokes an
immense sense of loss—all the more exasperating due to
our not being able to "see" the subtleties containing what
are perhaps the best sparks of the glittering energy of these
light coalescings of verse! To imagine the various extraor-
dinary occasions and extreme encounters that translation
takes from us, we need only think of the deft interplay in
haiku of ideograms and alphabetic signs.

   The transcription of the sounds of haiku into our own
alphabet—the results of which exert on the reader a strong
phonic grip and inspire a natural sympathy due to certain
vague affinities between the phonologies of Japanese and
Italian, allowing us to lovingly perceive certain consonances,
alliterations, syllabic symmetries—reveals how much is lost

*Andrea Zanzotto, "Prefazione," in *Cento haiku* (One hundred haiku), ed. and
trans. Irene Iarocci (Parma: Ugo Guanda Editore, 2010), 9–13 (a selection of
Japanese haiku translated into Italian; original edition published in 1982 by
Longanesi in Milan).

in the untranslatable word-pauses, roughly parallel to "men" and "de" in Ancient Greek, so valuable in their forthwith semantic "uselessness" and stupendous phatic halo.[1] The question then arises of how to render that "indistinct," or more to the point, "asubjective" essence that seems to pervade the Japanese language, for which every dative tends to settle into place, and then to rise into distinct relief, over a background of unconscious gray-blue in what seems a sign of "pure being," which in myriad definitions, or rather nondefinitions, is found in cultures throughout India and the Far East.

And what of more acute cultural shadings, such as how easy it is to lose your bearings simply because you *lack experience* of the fog as a sign of reality's well-being, as the visible, soft breathing of the landscape? And how do we find our way through the celebrations that give shape to the seasonal rhythms in haiku, celebrations so different from our own that the remembrance of the dead is observed, ever so wisely, during the most beautiful time of the year?

Gaping thus are the abysses, as unfathomable and inscrutable as they are irresistible, that haiku, in their swiftness, present to us westerners. Haiku shoot little blunted darts from a species of wonderland possessed of a subtle, intricate coherence that isn't simply the inversion of the mirror of our own coherences. Gyres that filter something blinding yet soothing, haiku are elastic cusps of a substance that remains hidden from us (and perhaps from everyone), but that we feel in some essential way is also our own. And thus in order to understand we fall back—at the very least—on a "principle of essentialness," on a theme of verbal economy

1. *Phatic,* of speech or speech sounds: serving to establish or maintain social relationships (or ineffable meaning) rather than to impart information.

that generates intense clustered tensions, or on a "fascina-
tion of the fragment," as though these were easily identifi-
able points of reference within the haiku tradition, even if
they instead have clear relationships with certain myths
and common beliefs in Western culture and poetry from the
late nineteenth and early twentieth centuries.

On the other hand, the fact that in Japan many themes
from the West have been accepted and developed in the
haiku tradition would seem to indicate that it isn't entirely
misguided to co-opt this poetic form within a certain arc
of Euro-American experience. Meaningful preludes cer-
tainly aren't lacking that lend credence to the validity of
the Western hallucination that for long has woven a literary
fabric composed of miscellaneous components from various
sources, characterized by concentration and intensity, that
together seem an amalgam of ruins and diamonds, ranging
from Japanese haiku to fragments of Greek (pre-Socratic)
lyrics. All these minimal forms, or rather forms condensed
to minimalism, were given meaning through an active re-
sidualism surviving within a crisis. "These fragments I have
shored against my ruins" might be the defining maxim of
this cultural trend, which by no means is yet exhausted.[2] On
the contrary, you need not look far to find ever new "com-
pulsions to repeat oneself," with glimmerings of fascinating
innovation, clear through to the most recent poetry. The
Japanese cultural presence, traceable as an iconological in-
fluence as early as the mid-nineteenth century, and later in
theater and literature, has been spread in no small measure
by the haiku tradition. Its impact has been most widely felt
in the work of poets working in English, from Ezra Pound
and William Carlos Williams to Conrad Aiken and Wallace

2. T. S. Eliot, *The Waste Land*.

Stevens, and groups such as the imagists, whose experiments opened the way to a vast and continuing creation of haiku by numerous enthusiasts (including the founding of groups such as the Haiku Society of America). And it would be remiss to overlook the form's influence on French poetry along a trajectory that includes Guillaume Apollinaire, Blaise Cendrars, and Paul Claudel, as well as Jean Cocteau, notably his theorizations of the "aesthetic of the minimal."

One might well wonder if there aren't echoes of haiku, more or less subterranean, in the unmistakable style of Giuseppe Ungaretti's early poetry, so striking at times are the affinities among formal tropes. In any case, the fact that the phenomenon is so widespread seems proof of a certain inescapable "fate"; the decontextualization of the haiku wasn't, it seems, an appropriation wholly uncalled for. And just as confidence in centralizing meaning was vanishing in the West—and increasingly along with it, any idea of a center—what better "fragment" than the haiku to indicate a space entirely fragmented and scattered?

There remains, beyond the problem of cultural nexuses, the unparalleled crispness of the haiku in its nearly precultural physicality, a structure marked by a primordial biorhythm, by an arsis and a thesis mesmerized by an ill-defined median suspension. There remains too the value of a sensitivity laden with intuitions, luminescent and capable, as Rudolf Arnheim has noted, of registering subtle chromatic and logical gradations—as if conjoined in a three-barrelled syrinx.[3] A breath of life rises up and seems to pass across it only once, but in returning in ever-new variations, prepares the ground for a fleeting, "tangential" union full

3. See Rudolf Arnheim, *Art and Visual Perception: A Psychology of the Creative Eye* (Berkeley: University of California Press, 2004).

of surprises and trembling inventions. Hovering like a flickering logos almost always free from the constrictions of a subject, it establishes the first inkling of a web from which are derived all the others. It is the initial contrivance of a "little mechanism" from which, with an almost sneaky obstinacy, there rises up an originary murmuring with relevance to more than poetry alone. If the *pointe* of the epigram, a rather elusive representation of radiant density, exhibits an aggressive and downright toxic character, the haiku instead with its never-conceited grace and budding delicacy presents as its *clou* a nonplace, a vague lack, a sweetly ritualized throbbing, the nonsound of the sense that opens into and embraces the nonsense of nature—because nature must "inhabit" the haiku in order to remain mother of all the senses.[4]

It is then fitting that Basho, the most respected innovator of the form, wished to root the haiku in a simple and "positive" concept of nature, which in turn is set free within the haiku according to the breezes peculiar to the seasons, each with its distinct hummings, colors, textures, sounds, heraldic animals, fruitings, crystallizations, precipitations. But within nature there is also an inscrutable muteness. And if the fact that the word suddenly falls silent befits the word, the exquisite, if somewhat bemused, savoring of a deep silence at the innermost recesses of the haiku is rendered possible by how quickly the word vanishes. Haiku seem rather apologetic for even existing, if existing entails any violence to "pure being" or to a "pure reader," if it entails a seduction so viscous as to risk seeming inelegant, or entails a game of logic that constricts or captures, rather than suddenly expanding in rousing utterance, in the blinking of eyes.

4. *Pointe* (French), tip, sharp end, (fig.) sharpness, pungency; *clou*, the point of greatest interest, the central idea.

There without doubt exists a danger of certain manner-isms in devotees—from an overzealous clinging to tradition, to an inflation of form—that by and large neglect the hai-ku's aura of economy, and risk degenerating into steriliza-tions characteristic of hyper-orthodoxy. But the restorative flow of haiku through our psyches, whether in swarms or one by one, today more than ever gives us signs of hope in the face of fetid abominations and ossifications—of nature, of humanity's capacity to feel and perceive—that are so much a part of current reality.

Translated by Patrick Barron

Selected Bibliography

POETRY

A che valse? (Versi 1938–1942). Milan: Scheiwiller, 1970.

La Beltà. Milan: Mondadori, 1968.

Conglomerati. Milan: Mondadori, 2009.

Dietro il paesaggio. Milan: Mondadori, 1951.

Elegia e altri versi. Milan: Gramigna, 1954.

Filò. Per il Casanova *di Fellini*. Milan: Mondadori, 1976.

Fosfeni. Milan: Mondadori, 1983.

Il Galateo in Bosco. Milan: Mondadori, 1978.

Gli Sguardi i Fatti e Senhal. Bernardi, 1969.

Idioma. Milan: Mondadori, 1986.

IX Ecloghe. Milan: Mondadori, 1962.

Ligonàs. Florence: Premio di Poesia Pandolfo, 1998.

Meteo. Rome: Donzelli, 1996.

Pasque. Milan: Mondadori, 1973.

Sovrimpressioni. Milan: Mondadori, 2001.

Vocativo. Milan: Mondadori, 1957.

CRITICISM, NARRATIVE, AND OTHER WRITING

Il cinema brucia e illumina: Intorno a Fellini e altri rari. Edited by Luciano De Giusti. Venice: Marsilio, 2011.

Colloqui con Nino. Parma: Edizioni Bernardi, 2005.

Racconti e prose. Milan: Mondadori, 1990.

Scritti sulla letteratura: Aure e disincanti nel Novecento letterario and *Fantasie di avvicinamento*. Edited by Gian Mario Villata. Milan: Mondadori, 2001.

Sull'Altopiano e prose varie. Vicenza: Neri Pozza, 1964.

EDITIONS

Poesie (1938–1986). Edited by Giorgio Luzzi. Turin: L'Arzanà, 1987.

Poesie (1938–1972). Edited by Stefano Agosti. Milan: Mondadori, 1973.

Le poesie e prose scelte. Edited by Stefano Dal Bianco and Gian Mario Villata. Milan: Mondadori, 1999.

Tutte le poesie. Edited by Stefano Dal Bianco. Milan: Mondadori, 2011.

EXTENDED INTERVIEWS

Eterna riabilitazione da un trauma di cui s'ignora la natura. Edited by Laura Barile and Ginevra Bompiani. Rome: Nottetempo, 2007.

In questo progresso scorsoio: Conversazione con Marzio Breda. Milan: Garzanti, 2009.

Ritratti: Andrea Zanzotto (DVD and book). Edited by Marco Paolini and Carlo Mazzacurati. Rome: Fandango Libri, 2006.

Viaggio musicale: Conversazioni a cura di Paolo Cattelan. Venice: Marsilio, 2008.

ENGLISH LANGUAGE TRANSLATIONS

Fosfeni. Translated by P. Verdicchio. Montreal: Guernica Editions, 2010.

Peasants Wake for Fellini's Casanova and Other Poems. Edited by

John P. Welle and Ruth Feldman. Chicago: University of
Illinois Press, 1997.

Poems by Andrea Zanzotto. Translated by Anthony Barnett.
Lewes: Allardyce, 1993.

The Selected Poetry and Prose of Andrea Zanzotto. Edited by
Patrick Barron. Chicago: University of Chicago Press,
2006.

The Selected Poetry of Andrea Zanzotto. Edited by Ruth Feldman
and Brian Swann. Princeton, NJ: Princeton University
Press, 1975.

STUDIES

Abati, Velio. *L'impossibilità della parola: Per una lettura
materialistica della poesia di Andrea Zanzotto.* Rome: Bagatto,
1991.

Agosti, Stefano. *Il testo poetico.* Milan: Rizzoli, 1972.

Albath-Folchetti, Maike. *Zanzottos Triptychon: Eine Studie
der Sammlungen "Il Galateo in Bosco," "Fosfeni," und "Idioma."*
Tübingen: Gunter Narr, 1998.

Allen, Beverly. *Andrea Zanzotto: The Language of Beauty's
Apprentice.* Berkeley: University of California Press, 1988.

Autografo (*I Novanta di Zanzotto: Studi, incontri, lettere,
immagini*), no. 46. Novara: Interlinea, 2011.

Bertini, Lucia Conti. *Andrea Zanzotto o la sacra menzogna.*
Venice: Marsilio, 1984.

Calabretto, Roberto, ed. *Andrea Zanzotto: Tra musica, cinema e
poesia.* Udine: Forum Editrice, 2005.

Carbognin, Francesco, ed. *Andrea Zanzotto: Un poeta nel tempo.*
Bologna: Edizioni Aspasia, 2008.

Carbognin, Francesco. *"L'altro spazio": Scienza, paesaggio, corpo
nella poesia di Andrea Zanzotto.* Varese: Nuova Magenta, 2007.

Conti Bertini, Lucia. *Andrea Zanzotto o la sacra mensogna.*
Venice: Marsilio, 1984.

Dal Bianco, Stefano. *Tradire per amore: La metrica del primo Zanzotto 1938–1957*. Lucca: Maria Pacini Fazzi, 1997.

Falchetta, Piero. *Oculus Pudens: Venti anni di poesia di Andrea Zanzotto (1957–1978)*. Padua: Abano Terme: 1983.

Hand, Vivienne. *Zanzotto*. Edinburgh: Edinburgh University Press, 1994.

L'immaginazione. Issues 37–38 (January–February 1987), 175 (February–March 2001), and 230 (May 2007). San Cesario di Lecce: Editore Piero Manni.

Lensia, Maria Grazia. *Il segno trasgressivo (Giorgio Bàrberi Squarotti e Andrea Zanzotto)*. Foggia: Bastogi, 1990.

Manica, Raffaele, ed. *Omaggio a Zanzotto per i suoi ottanta anni*. Manziana: Vecchiarelli, 2001.

Motta, Uberto. *Ritrovmenti di senso nella poesia di Zanzotto*. Milan: Vita e Pensiero, 1996.

Nimis, Jean. *"Un processus de verbalisation du monde": Perspectives du sujet lyrique dans la poésie d'Andrea Zanzotto*, Berne: Peter Lang, 2006.

Nuvoli, Giuliana. *Andrea Zanzotto*. Florence: La Nuova Italia, 1979.

Parise, Goffredo and Giosetta Fioroni. *Tapestry: Psyche, metapsiche e guerre stellari*. Mantua: Maurizio Corrani, 1992.

Pezzin, Claudio. *Zanzotto e Leopardi: Il poeta come infans*. Verona: Cooperativa Editrice Nuova Grafica Cierre, 1988.

Piangatelli, Roberto. *La lingua il corpo il bosco: La poesia di Andrea Zanzotto*. Macerata: Verso, 1990.

Pizzamiglio, Giberto. *Andrea Zanzotto: Tra Soligo e laguna di Venezia*. Venice: Leo S. Olschki, 2008.

Prammer, Theresia. *Lesarten der Sprache: Andrea Zanzotto in deutschen Übersetzungen*. Würzburg: Verlag Königshausen & Neumann, 2005.

Sartori, Enio. *Tra bosco e non bosco*. Macerata: Quodlibet, 2010.

Spampinato, Graziella. *La musa interrogata: L'opera in versi e in prosa di Andrea Zanzotto*. Milan: Hefti, 1996.

Stefanelli, Luca. *Attraverso la beltà di Andrea Zanzotto: Macrotesto, intertestualità, ragioni genetiche*. Pisa: Edizioni ETS (Studi di critica e filologia), 2011.

Tassoni, Luigi. *Caosmos: La poesia di Andrea Zanzotto*. Rome: Carrocci, 2002.

Tassoni, Luigi. *Sogno del caos: "Microfilm" di Andrea Zanzotto e la geneticità del testo*. Bergamo: Moretti & Vitali, 1990.

Villalta, Gian Mario. *La costanza del vocativo: Lettura della "trilogia" di Andrea Zanzotto; Il Galateo in bosco, Fosfeni, Idioma*. Milan: Guerini, 1992.

Waterhouse, Peter. *Im Genesis: Gelände; Versuch über einige Gedichte von Paul Celan und Andrea Zanzotto*. Basel-Weil am Rhein-Wien, 1997.

Welle, John P. *The Poetry of Andrea Zanzotto: A Critical Study of Il galateo in bosco*. Rome: Bulzoni, 1987.

Index of First Lines